Take Home Poems

A Third Collection of Poetry

by
Matt. Meyers

© Matt. Meyers
1995
All Rights Reserved

Please Address Book Orders and Correspondence to:

Matt. Meyers
HC-66, Box 109
Hillsboro, N.M. 88042

Printed on recycled paper, with soy-based ink
By Thomson-Shore Inc. Dexter, Michigan.

Typeset by Sans Serif, Ann Arbor, Michigan.

Cover design by Ann Lowe.

Library of Congress Catalogue Number 95-90080

ISBN 0-9646336-0-4

For Samuel and Carolyn Meyers

radiant hearts
loving beings
parents

For Larry Rosenberg and Thich Nhat Hanh

teachers of meditation

And for Melinda Sue Madix

beloved friend

Acknowledgements

I am grateful to the editors of the following publications, who first printed some of the poems appearing in this book:

"Pulsars", *The Connection*, Arivaca, Arizona, 1993

"Homage To The Pecan", "Sacrament", "Whole Coconut", "Golf Course", "Fake Food", "In Defiance of Math", *Hygienic Community Network Newsletter*, Sun City, Arizona, 1993–1994

"Chem Lawn", *Our Toxic Times*, White Sulphur Springs, Montana, 1994

"Pesticides", *EcoLife*, Rio Rancho, New Mexico, November, 1994

"Dance", *Asheville Poetry Review*, Autumn, 1994

Travel Log

Arad, Israel
Aravaca, Arizona

Gray trees
Greet arid wind
Under one sun
Flickering.

Train Town

It's good to live in a town
Where a freight-train stops traffic
In a moment's notice like now.

It's good to live in a town
Where the train whistles themes
Of forests, mists, streams
Of hobos hitching
Freedom from being bogged down.

It's good to live in a town
Where a long train lumbers through at noon
Slicing the heat tumbling wind
With increased slowing down.

Shreveport, Louisiana
Monday, 8 A.M.

Smokestack.
Traffic Jam.
A black man
Pushes a broken cadillac
Off the On ramp.

Near Happy, Texas

Lone Star State
Flag flapping in gray wind.
Fatigue. Cold.
Old old wandering.

Texas Outback

Route 86 heading North and West.
Red clay cliffs.
Good loneliness.

From Texas Into New Mexico

This trip seems pre-lived;
As if I am catching up
With a previously written script.

I breeze.
I am doing little
of the steering.

New Mexican Outback

You spend the whole day not seeing a soul.
Not even seeing a human being.

Storm

In the mountains
The winds come fierce and fast.
Unannounced.
And then they pass.

So why fear wind?
Why even fear chance?

Live naturally.
Lash yourself to a tree.
This storm is our dance.
This limb is our destiny.

Along A Nearby Creek

Slowly I trek along a nearby creek
Marveling at trees reaching straight-up
Dunking my scalp
into falls of cold run-off
Listening to melodies the creek makes
Its constant dropping towards Down and In,
Singing songs without words
Or with words I do not yet fathom.

I must not greed beyond this creek.
I need to take in its healing.

In A Circle Of Sun

How long the path
And brief the moment.
To be free of low commotion.

East Cide, West Cide

Autumnal

It's autumn and I can't keep from sighing:
Planet Earth are you really dying?
Will there be a Spring
After this year's pesticide spraying?

How much poison can you absorb
Before you break down and uncontrollably sob,
Rip out your hair, tear your flowered dress
Wretch with earthquakes and pestilence.

Chem Lawn

Most of the trees have been cut down.
The choice organic air is gone.
Instead there are lawns.
Polluted parcels of termite control
Poisoned grass on which pets and children roll
Scorched earth
Bearing no edible fruit.

On A Manicured Lawn

On a manicured lawn
A house cat goes into a convulsive fit.
Saliva drips from her locked jaw.
The lawn is well watered.

Golf Course

The golf course is a buzz
With lawn mowers and chemical applicators.
It takes five men three hours
To keep one putting green green.
This is obscene.

They could be planting collards
Or almond trees.

Before The Chemical Industry

Before the chemical industry
Got their products into everything,
An apple used to be an apple
And trees were trees.

Now an apple is a food-grade shellac
And trees are a "renewable forest product".

It's a shame.
There ought to be a law.
Write to Congress
And tell him or her
You want to know
The taste of a tomato.

Even The Ocean

Even the ocean has been sterilized.
It no longer smells from fish or kelp
barnacles or sea vegetables.

Grace

Yellow apple
golden like the sun.

Dear grower
keep it from harm.

Keep it from poison
and from poisoning.

Sacrament

This banana comes from a "foreign" land
Laced with pesticides
That kill women and men.

Choose well.
Do not ingest poisonous chemicals.

Pesticides

The food we eat is despised by flies.
Raccoons won't touch store-bought plums.
Why this self-poisoning?
Why not insist on nutritional justice?

Buy organic.

Fake Food

It looks like a banana but it is not.
They look like oranges and apples and carrots
But they are ersatz.

Our store bought fruits and vegetables
have been zapped,
By infertile chemicals and toxic "cides"
And gases to hasten "ripening"
And waxes, shellacs, and dyes.

No wonder our nation lacks
vitality, and seeks energy
from doctors, fads, caffeine.

Our soil and our blood have been
weakened and dis-eased
By agrochemical "food" and impostor greens.

Doctors Root and Clay

The earth is our healer
Bearing doctors named root and clay.
She has foraged for us
Amongst rocks and seas
Remedies that heal for free.

Search peacefully.
Spare dandelion.
Do not on "weeds" spray poison.

The Wealth of Our Nation

The wealth of our nation does not come from
Wall Street or Main Street
or from computer screens;
Or from betting on the future price
Of coffee, sugar, or soybeans.

The wealth of our nation
Comes from the soil we farm,
The food we eat
The water we drink
The air we breathe.

To be rich we must invest
In shovel and compost heap,
Rotting lettuce leaves
That will make our crops and blood
Resistant to disease.

Morsels

To Survive

To survive
The industrial race will have to learn
To vegetate.
To become more simple and alive
More plant like.

Polemic

Eat more than one organic apple a day
To keep the plethora of specialists away.

Kasha, Communion

The body of the mother spirit
I take in.
I eat the wafer of the loyal feminine
in the groat, the herb,
the brown kernal of life
that smiles.
Of Earth.

Homage To The Pecan

Little brain encased within a wooden skull.
I am grateful to savour and to digest
Your brace and your intelligence.

Another Sacrament

This banana comes from a "foreign" land
Via many poor and noble hands.

Love well.
Our nourishment is a miracle.

Whole Coconut

Digestible milk
for the human adult.

Untainted meat
Hygienic and complete.

Three Porridges

Quinoa

Humble seed
The energy you give
Propels large muscles.
Keeps me alive
Inspires.

Millet

Dear God thank you
For this simple food.
This warmth
This porridge.

Teff

It has the color of Ethiopia.
It is a tiny brown seed.
May it help us to wean
From meat, from greed.

Garden Solitude

My laugh has taken on the cadence of doves.
I am very easily influenced.
Flowers open to the morning sun.
A purple herb inside me blooms.

Fruits of the Elders

May the fruits of the elders be sweet.
May they eat sweet melons
in the ripeness of their time.
May their happiness bloom.
May their shoes be filled with the steps
of grateful children.
May harmony follow them
for seven generations.

May they, in this life, rest in peace.

In A Moment of Peace

In A Moment Of Peace

In a moment of peace
Are all the seasons
And all the reasons
For being alive.
In a moment of peace
Is a tiny flower
And the Universe
Behind closed eyes.
In a moment of peace
Is the quiver of being
The peace of no demise.

No Boundaries

Where are the boundaries of the Spring?

Between wind and leaf.
Sun and budding.

In The Desert

In the desert I whiff green farm.
The occasional breeze of ocean.
The earth, we are one
Breath, stone, pilgrim.

In A Dream

In a dream I asked if there was a God
And the answer came back "Yes
And his name is Joel Fleisher
And he pushes a cart.

And each night he silently empties it,
With sky pouring out from the sides".

Flu In Jerusalem

For the whole day
I've watched God inside of me
Make antibodies.

Fever, aches,
Rising and setting sun,
God is One.

Sabbath Is A Convalescence

Sabbath is a convalescence.
Depleted, we need more
Than one Sabbath a week,
More than one retreat a year,
More than one moment of silence.

Guide Me

Guide me, O Jehovah
On my journey through
this thick green dream.
Guide me through
this long night life,
This haunting reed-singing.

Guide me to your eternity
To unite with Mother Marie.

Pulsars

Our hearts are pulsing
Our minds are pulsing
With unseen pulsing stars.
We are pulsars in a velvet sky
A part.

Forest Web

Reminders of life.
Reminders of death.
One consciousness.
One breath.

Untitled

In a vast mountain range
The sound of one bird
Confirms silence.

I Cannot Own

I cannot own a gate or a tree.
I float past them
And them past me.

In Defiance of Math

At the creek bed dragon flies mate.
Joined in summer
One plus one equals one.
And if successful
One plus one equals three
Or three thousand, or three million.

Arithmetic is not supreme fact.
One, like white light, contains all.
So does None.

When I Feel Fine

When I feel fine
bricks piled on top of a wooden picnic table
in the rain or sunshine
become high art.

Every steamed leaf of collard greens
becomes a delicious treat.
Every natural phenomena
all hues of blending green
become a source a peace.

When I feel fine
After a morning of strong meditation
The past passes gently by
happy to be moving on.

When I feel fine, I am content to stay put
      or to travel,
Not needing to appropriate
the lush forest as mine.

Thanksgiving (Late November)

The majority of leaves have fallen.
The flutter is over.
Now it is cloudy.
One leaf at a time.
Silent.

December Silence

This month is of silence.
The silence of trees
when there is no wind,

The culmination silence
of Christmas Eve
When all may rest in peace.

Desert Dusk

Desert dusk.
Night birds chirping
Do not disturb
A descending calm.

Before Dawn, I Ask Myself

What if today the sun does not rise?

Are you ready to embrace
The serenity of space?

Day

The light of many stars
Becomes One.

Rope Dance

Dance

Outside, beyond the curtain of sand
Trees laugh.
This life is a phantom's dance.
Ghosts and friends hold hands, pass.

We jig.
We are in a unison
way beyond our fathoming.
We arise. We pant.
We are organelles in a green blood's dance.

The caller is fast.
He slurs "tobacco, cattle, teachers, chance".
We are partners in a green blood's dance.

Silent Night

On Christmas Eve
Custodial workers clean
offices on Wall Street.

Quietly they go about their chores.
Vacuum carpets, tidy desks, sweep floors.

This has been a week of many drunken parties.
But tonight the offices are quiet
Cubes of light within a sober night.

The workers meditate on sacrifice.

Sarajevo

Our innocence is unable to protect
The victim of today's hot bullet.

But why?
Is there some large un-collected debt
That we owe to our past?
Some hidden balance due
Payable in the war dance?

When fate needs bodies
to place before the wall
It chooses us all.
Victim, killer, observer,
In unison we fall.

Warmth

We began in Kenya, or the womb
And then lumbered on
to where it is cold.

But warmth remains
a requirement of our bones.
The warmth of friends
the warmth of food
the warmth of clothes,
Solaces
On our way home.

After The Storm

After the storm
A rainbow.
Arching high
Over my neighbor
and I.

Come Sweet Elder

Come sweet elder
Lay down in our pasture.
With grey horse
And shade tree
You've earned gentle company.

The Heart Sermon

Between the head and the gut
is the heart.
And between the heart and the heart
is Love.
The unthinking power, the freedom.

Rope Dance

Such a beautiful fit
our love makes.
Like a woven rope:
Unafraid to Unafraid.

Other Books of Poetry by Matt. Meyers

Peace Proceeds In Glimpses, 1988

In Search of Silence, 1992

Are Available From:

Venus in Libra Books
HC-66
Box 109
Hillsboro, NM 88042